Early Retirement: An Indian Perspective

Acknowledgments

The last few years have been challenging for the majority of us due to the pandemic. The pandemic changed the way we looked at our lives and priority. We all are more conscious of unforeseen situations now than we were ever before. Many of us have brought many positive changes to our lives and the community around us.

During these years, I spent a lot of time with my son – Adhrith. Spending time with him gave me immense joy. It was during one of my evening walks with him, I got struck with the idea of writing this book.

As I have further written about savings and investments in my book, I always considered investments as a guiding force for wealth generation but had little understanding of savings. My wife Parul with little knowledge of investments has always been a staunch believer in the power of savings. I learned the importance and basic tenets of savings from her. She has her methods of savings which are very effective. It took me a lot of time to be on the savings side but thanks to her that now I am on.

The basics of investments, compounding, the world of mutual funds, and the equity market were exposed to me by my father at a very early stage. This early exposure has helped me in pursuing my career in the investment world.

Lastly, my friend Vinayak has been a great help while I was writing this book. Despite being busy with his work schedule, he helped me thanklessly.

Contents

Chapter 1: Why Early Retirement?

Chapter 2: What to consider for Retirement?
 > 3Ms Method

Chapter 3: Planning for early retirement
  > Saving mindset for early retirement

Chapter 4: Building Retirement Corpus
  > 25x Rule
  > First Corpus
  > Second Corpus
  > Assumptions
  > Constituents of Retirement Kitty
  > Identifying a good mutual fund
  > Summary of Contributions and expected corpus

Chapter 5: Questions?

Chapter 6: Onset of Retirement
  > At Early Retirement
  > At Usual Retirement

Chapter 7: Finally

Why Early Retirement?

We all love Fridays but hate Mondays. The dread of returning to work on Monday begins on Sunday evening when we are preparing ourselves to return to a job many of us dislike.

Early retirement can free us from this. Many of us chose the job solely because it supports our living and maintains our lifestyle.

One can still pick another job based on interests rather than remuneration. It may be a hobby, charity, volunteering, a low-paying job, or going back to basics in the agriculture or art field. The idea is to create an ecosystem of psychological strength and savings to survive the rest of life without working regular 9-5 jobs. Financial freedom means being free of typical and self-imposed jobs; it defies the usual way of living and defies following the crowd. On the other hand, psychological freedom relates to freeing oneself from unnecessary lifestyle expenses.

This book aims to guide people to think and plan for their financial and psychological freedom. While the broader principles apply to everyone, this book is aimed at Indians living in or outside India. This book assumes they would like to stay in India after early retirement. The whole idea around early retirement is not sitting idle but doing something for reduced hours in a day or week. And this new hobby cum job should be interesting enough to engage one for a long time. So, one should do something which one can do without worrying about an income from the job.

This book further covers various financial aspects of early retirement, including how to build a retirement corpus, consider retirement homes, medical facilities, financial support, freedom, and inflation. This may not cover individual scenarios but will help anyone begin formulating their plan. Let's discuss various aspects of early retirement in detail.

What to consider for Retirement?

The main factors to consider include housing, the cost of social and medical support, emergencies, and loss of life and property. Let's discuss some of these factors.

Inflation has impacted all of us. We have lost the value of money due to rises in the price of commodities, goods, and services. Let's consider how inflation generally impacts early retirement. It's important to first consider general inflation, such as the cost of goods and services, including increases in the cost of houses, vehicles, food, fuel, and daily items.

We can minimize the impact of inflation on early retirement by fixing some of these costs. For example, if you buy your retirement house early, an increase in real estate costs won't impact you. You may see some impact of inflation on the maintenance cost of your house, but it won't be nearly as high as the cost of a house.

You will need a place to live comfortably for the rest of your life. A **retirement house** could be your current house if you plan to stay in smaller cities or a purpose-bought retirement house. A cost-benefit analysis can also help when buying a property for retirement. This can be far from the city or it could be in your hometown. In terms of cost, it is always good to buy a house in a suburban area since they are cheaper. It is better to buy while you are still earning rather than just before your early retirement. The two benefits of this are a lower real estate cost and the development of facilities between accumulation and early retirement.

It will be your personal preference whether you want to buy a flat or a house. But the key is to spend less money and look for smaller spaces as they require less maintenance in terms of cost and effort. You can buy or build your retirement house in Coimbatore instead of Chennai, Mysore instead of Bengaluru, Pune suburban instead of Mumbai, Lucknow instead of Delhi, Ranikhet instead of Mussoorie, or Bhubaneshwar instead of Kolkata. This decision should be based on your climate, culture, and facility availability preferences. The goal is to eliminate the expenses of bigger cities and move to smaller cities with lower expenses. The smaller cities are similar to the metro in terms of facilities.

In terms of **vehicles**, always choose the car that suits your needs and has a lower cost of maintenance and ownership. It is important to reduce spending on assets whose value will decrease over time. Cars are depreciating assets, meaning their value will go down unless it is a vintage car. Consider your current perspective on buying a fancy or bigger car. Smaller, more efficient, and safe cars are always ideal for early retirement. If a change in market regulation for vehicles or new engine types occurs, wait for the right time and right price to switch. For example, switching from petrol/diesel/CNG to an electric car is currently unideal due to the high cost of electric vehicles. Once the price of the car drops, you can consider buying a new one.

An often ignored form of inflation is the **medical** kind. Medical inflation is generally two or three times higher than general inflation. What can we do to reduce the financial burdens of medical inflation? The approach towards health should be preventive instead of curative. This means using healthy habits to avoid disease. For example, consider doing a basic set of exercises daily. Focus on doing such practices consistently rather than doing long hours of exercise on a few occasions. However, for unexpected medical emergencies, it's important to have comprehensive health insurance. You can have a look at some of the criteria used for identifying a health insurance policy in the chapter – 'Building Retirement Corpus'.

Walking, getting proper sleep, and eating healthy foods are some of the best things you can do. If you take precautions to avoid an unhealthy lifestyle, you could save yourself a lot of financial and psychological burdens. Aim to eat organic food and consider growing some vegetables in your kitchen garden. Remember, you can always grow something on your balcony or rooftop if your house is small. Organic food is costly, but it has worthwhile long-term benefits. While you may be unable to eat entirely organic foods, try to eat as many as possible. Instead of eating junk and street food, limit these for your long-term health.

3Ms Method:

There are several principles that one should always be mindful of. These are some of the universal and omnipresent ideas in all societies to make one worthy of accumulating wealth. Unless you are conscious of these ideas in your heart and action, being wealthy is a difficult task. But once you have mastered these in your actions, these will turn out to be torch bearers in the journey of wealth creation. The reason I am talking about wealth creation here is that this wealth creation will bring out the required financial freedom for your early retirement.

3Ms method is the core combination of 3 principles that drives the idea of wealth generation. The three Ms (3M) are **M**aximum Savings, **M**anaging Risk, and **M**agic of compounding.

Maximum Savings

Maximum savings as a term is very subjective and depends from person to person. The maximum savings could vary based on one's present financial condition, personal, family, and social obligations, and mindset. Maximum saving is driven by how one perceives it. Saving and being thrifty is the only sure-shot way of accumulating wealth. The idea of maximum savings revolves around being conscious of one's spending. The spending should be in line with one's needs. It can be achieved by a mindset that always looks for an additional bit of savings.

At the execution level, the two main acts of savings and investments are two different subjects. The majority of people tend to be good at one of these two and to a good extent, they wish to be good at the later one. But wishing and being good at investing won't be of much help unless you are good at savings. One has to be better with both of these two activities. The ideal is to be very good at savings and to be not bad at investments. Working on the savings looks boring and time taking while investments as an activity look thrilling and rewarding. This is more of a perception and leads to confusing results. Saving is the bitter and the most fundamental truth of wealth creation.

Savings does not require any technical knowledge, it requires perseverance and discipline. As I said earlier, we Indians are gifted in being thrifty and having a saving mindset. In the last few decades, we have lost it to the glitter of modernity. A generation before, this saving mindset was a way of life and a common sense where people lived within their means and saved for the future.

Similarly, Investments also need common sense. We have to always rely on simpler investment avenues and simpler products. Complex products bring complexity and additional risks. Such products come with a cost, sometimes the cost is hidden. Always buy an investment product from an institution specialized and reputed in that space.

Avoid buying an investment product from a life insurance company. A life insurance company is meant to sell insurance products not investments. Investments are a function of an asset management company or an investment management company. Many of us are aware of these facts but somehow feel tied up with our past commitments. We need to avoid such mistakes in their entirety.

Managing Risks

Risk is just a term for everybody unless one meets it face to face. Our mind always looks for validation and pretends that an inherent risk will not occur in our case. But the risk is real and it brings immense pain especially when it causes financial instability. So, we have to be mindful of the risk and the damage it can cause to our financial position. Here, we are only talking about the risk which we come across during our investment lifecycle. Managing risk is necessary for wealth creation and it is a must for early retirement.

Risk has to be managed as it cannot be avoided completely. It includes identifying the risk, assessing and quantifying the risk, and finally treating the risk. One should always be aware of the potential risks and probability of their occurrence. It's always a good idea to take a certain level of risk and avoid a few of them. Risk is associated with reward. It is said that the more risk you take, the more reward it has for you. This may be true in the majority of the cases but not always. There are two things to keep in mind – one, what is the gravity of loss in case a risk arises. The second is what is the occurrence and frequency of the risk.

There are four major combinations of risk occurrence and frequency. One - A risk could bear less loss but could occur frequently while in 2nd case, the risk could bear more loss but could occur less frequently. The third one is where both gravity and frequency of loss are higher and the fourth one is where both gravity and frequency of loss are low.

If you look at the above four, you can easily figure out that the third combination is what we need to avoid and the fourth combination is ideal for us. But we need to remember that in the case of the fourth combination, the probability of gain is also less. So, we have to look for such a combination of risk gravity and occurrence but should not completely rely on this for wealth gain. Instead, we should also explore the number one and two combinations.

We should not take a risk unless we understand the gravity of risk, its impact, and especially when we cannot quantify its impact. It is also essential to take certain risk but it has to be calculated.

Magic of Compounding

"The magic of compounding interest is truly the eighth wonder of the world!"

— Albert Einstein

It is said that in the investment world, there is only one magic – compounding, the rest all are tricks. The tricks may or may not work in your favor but the magic of compounding will always work for your good. This magic does not require you to invest your money in any fancy and complex financial instruments, this works even in simpler instruments. The magic lies in earning interest on each interest earned in past.

For retirement, let's take an example -

If one is at the age of 25 years, put Rs 1 lac lump sum in any good equity mutual funds for another 35 years i.e. to receive the amount at the retirement age of 60 years. Let's assume the rate of interest is 15% compounded annually. Can you guess how much this maturity amount be? It will be Rs 1.33 Cr. Isn't it huge? Even if you become a bit conservative and put the rate of interest to be 12% which is achievable in 35 years, the maturity amount will be around 52 Lacs. Though Rs 1.33 Cr and Rs 52 lacs are big amounts today they may not be as worthy in 35 years but still see how much corpus can be created. This is the magic of compounding.

It just needs two things – early investment and patience. We should never disturb the compounding by buying/selling instruments frequently. High transaction costs will create a huge difference over a long period of time.

Planning for early retirement

If you are considering early retirement, you should start planning as soon as possible. Instead of putting your money into random asset classes, invest it in certain buckets and maintain these.

For typical retirement, most people save at least 20% of their income. However, for early retirement, one has to save double of this amount.

Saving mindset for early retirement

You can save a lot by putting off unnecessary expenses. It is said that earning more money is easier than saving more money. We live in a world where our spending is driven by fear of how others will judge us. Additionally, materialism has a profound impact on our lives. The intended result of materialism is happiness, and this materialistic happiness is a combination of true happiness plus the happiness generated by being admired by others. Consider the happiness someone feels while on holiday on a beach. This is amplified merely by the thought of posting pictures of it on social media. Can one live without putting pictures on social media? Yes, but it's difficult for the majority of people.

Saving is not rocket science; it is common sense. This sense has been with Indians for generations. By nature, we are thrifty and focused on savings. Modern world economies encourage and stimulate us to buy things. Based on this consumerism, the world's developed economies have grown and impacted us. Living in the present is the new mantra. So, how do we control ourselves? It could be as simple as asking ourselves at every financial transaction: how is this transaction going to add value or simplify my life, and for how long?

Here are a few ways you can save some money. Remember, any saved rupee should go into your early retirement kitty:

1. If you don't need it, don't buy it. If you are considering buying something, just wait for another 3 days. After these 3 days, ask yourself again if you need it. The majority of the time, if it is not something you need, you will be able to avoid spending the money.
2. Many people justify their spending by saying they are buying a quality product. Ask yourself if this is the reason, or if is it part of the latest trend you want to show off. Never buy the newest version of products, especially electronics, unless you need the new features. For example, buy an older version of the iPhone instead of the latest model. Quality-wise, they are about the same.
3. There are a few items you should avoid buying new, such as books. The value of such items won't increase or decrease whether it is new or old. Always sell such things after your usage and put any extra money in your retirement kitty.
4. Don't celebrate modern celebration days like Mother's Day or Father's Day; instead, celebrate only birthdays. Also, ignore sales days associated with such celebrations organized by malls and online retailers.
5. Review your subscriptions and cancel the ones you don't use. You can always rejoin, and these days, there is no penalty for cancellation. Put the money saved in your early retirement kitty.
6. Use the cashback website for online shopping and add any cashback to your retirement kitty.
7. Don't travel business class or premium, instead opting for economy class while flying. Similarly, don't travel in first class or tier 2 class; travel in tier 3 while traveling by train. You can have a quality travel experience without choosing the top-notch classes.
8. Never buy yearly subscriptions for gyms and clubs unless you are confident that you will use the services for the whole year. Start with monthly

options and select a longer duration contract when you show up consistently.
9. Reinvest any dividends from your stocks or funds into the same stock and fund. If you don't reinvest this dividend, this dividend money gets lost in day-to-day expenses. It is advisable to go for the growth option of mutual funds unless receiving dividends has a tax benefit or you otherwise need dividend income. Also, consider reinvesting this income into your retirement fund.
10. When buying a car for personal use, don't buy the top variant of the car of a particular model. Instead, look for variants that are worth the money. Always do the comparison and chose the car that has the necessary feature you are looking for. Also, consider the total cost of ownership instead of the upfront cost. Often, the total cost of ownership is much more than the upfront cost.
11. Look for a better deal for your existing home loan or ask your existing home loan provider about a reduction in the interest rate. These days, banks increase the interest rate due to changes in their base rate, and won't reduce your interest rate unless you ask. Any reduction in your monthly EMI should go straight into your retirement kitty. Also, the process is usually easier to take a home loan from a private bank, but the rate of interest is a few basis points higher than that offered by public sector banks. However, you can always move to a lower interest offered by public sector banks later. This may look like a hassle initially, but once you have transferred from a higher interest rate to a lower interest rate, it makes a big difference over the long term as the loan ticket size is generally large. Put any saved rupee in your retirement kitty.
12. Buy quality products in smaller quantities and use all of them. Though it may be costly upfront, you will save more in the long term.

These are among the ways you could have additional savings and channel them towards your retirement corpus. Remember, these are not the only ways; you may have your ways of saving money. These could be entirely different from what I have listed above. The objective of listing these points is to urge you to be thrifty and considerate in your spending and put any additional savings in your retirement fund.

When you save something but you are not investing it into your retirement funds, it will get lost in overall expenses and you will not even notice you saved it. You will never see these savings impact your future in a big way. Always keep a track of such savings and put them to work by investing them.

Building Retirement Corpus

The first question that often comes to our mind is how much money we will need for our retirement. There is no straightforward answer to this but a properly defined framework could help in that direction. We will discuss the contours of such a framework.

Several websites and methods can be used for setting a corpus, but having too many options may become confusing. As long as you are aware and have accounted for inflation affecting to cost of living in your decision-making, the ballpark number should set the stage.

The retirement corpus has to be carefully considered while designing the early retirement portfolio. You need at least 12 to 15 years for the accumulation of corpus. It is difficult to create your early retirement corpus unless you have a lot of money from an inheritance or other sources if you are planning to accumulate in less than 10 years. If your accumulation period is less than 15 years, early retirement could be difficult.

25x Rule

There are several methods through which corpus can be calculated. We will use the '25x Rule' for building a retirement corpus. This method is simple and accepted throughout the world. While it is designed for the USA, it suits India as well due to the predictability of one's income and inflation. We will use this formula to calculate the corpus but we will make some adjustments to the withdrawal rules. If we use our withdrawals conservatively, the corpus will be sufficient to last one's life. The confidence in the sufficiency of corpus comes primarily from the nature of the Indian economy which is in the developing stage. It is growing at a healthy rate and is expected to move in that direction for several decades. This has effectively created an opportunity to earn a handsome rate of return.

Let's say you already have your own house and earn a salary of 100,000 Rs per month (post-tax and EPF contribution) and your current monthly expenses are 40,000 Rs per month. The expenses total 4.8 Lacs per year. If you plan to retire around the age of 45 and your current age is 30, this means you have another 15 years for accumulation.

We will use the above current age, expense, and early retirement age as a baseline to discuss various aspects of early retirement throughout this book. Any figures or sums will evolve around the above example. You can always tweak the above numbers and further calculations to your circumstances. However, these broad principles will remain the same for anyone.

So, we need to calculate your potential expenses at the age of 45. We should have a ballpark number based on inflation. If we predict average inflation of 4%, next year's expenses will be 4.99 Rs (4.8 Lacs + (4.8 lacs * 4%)). Therefore, an increase of 4% every year will lead to an expense of around 8.65 Lacs after 15 years.

Now, we have some idea of our expenses after 15 years; this is not exact but should be used as a guideline. Now, we can apply the '25x rule'. The retirement corpus needed at age 45 will be 2.15 Cr Rs. This corpus has been calculated by multiplying 8.65 Lacs by 25. So, in this scenario, one has to have 2.15 Cr Rs. as retirement corpus at the age of 45. If the same person wants to retire today, he/she will need 1.2 Cr Rs. We are assuming that he/she does not have this much money, so they can aim for creating a corpus of 2.15 Cr. It is assumed that one already has some money saved for this purpose.

Let's find out how much one needs to save to reach this corpus. There are two steps to achieving this – the first is a lump sum investment of 15 lacs for the next 15 years, and assuming the expected rate of return is 12%, this value will grow to 90 Lacs after 15 years. The 2nd step is a systematic investment of 25000 Rs per month for 15 years in a good equity fund. At the expected interest rate of 12%, this totals 1.25 Cr. The total corpus of the lump sum investment plus the sum of systematic investment equals 2.15 Cr Rs. We are aiming for this sum as our early retirement corpus for the given scenario.

This is a very simplistic way of looking at corpus creation, but later in this book, we will split this 25000 Rs per month investment across various investment avenues like PPF, NPS, and Mutual Funds. We will also make changes to these numbers to make them more practical. For example, investing a lump sum amount of Rs 15 lacs for 15 years only for retirement purposes may not be possible for someone in a similar situation as the example. So, we will make various adjustments to allow the approach to be useful and pragmatic.

Through the '25x' rule, we determined the overall corpus needed for early retirement, but we will modify it to make it conservative enough to achieve. As part of this modification, the key is to break the retirement corpus into two parts. The first one is needed for early retirement at the age of 45. The other is for the usual retirement age of around 60.

The purpose of these two sets of the corpus is to ensure that about half of the contribution is invested for another 15 years to allow for compounding. Both corpora have a core and a peripheral investment avenue, balancing the need for capital protection and inflation-adjusted returns.

First Corpus

This is meant to be ready after 15 years. Though the time frame of 15 years is considered long-term, we have to prepare for any unforeseen situations, especially any prolonged lull in market conditions. So, we are keeping this in 2 constituents – Public Provident Fund (PPF) and Mutual Funds (SIPs and Lumsum Investments). The contribution in PPF will ensure that capital protection and the core of corpus are maintained. Though there could be fluctuations in interest rates, PPF returns will remain decent and consistent for a given year or quarter. As PPF is government-backed, this is a safer investment and, for retirement purposes, is what we are looking for.

While PPF corpus is on the safer side, we need to have something that can bring superior returns, particularly in terms of beating inflation. We will go with Mutual Funds via the Systematic Investment and lump sum investment route. In the history of the Indian Equity market, it has been observed that over 10-15 years, equities have offered one of the best returns, especially during the periods of economic growth in India. We will go into detail about fund selections and how much one needs to contribute in later chapters.

Second Corpus

We are creating this corpus for the usual retirement age, and we are assuming this will be at age 60. This means that any contribution to this corpus could have a maximum investment timeframe of 30 years. For this corpus, we intend to only have contributions for the first 15 years, after which point we intend to take early retirement. There won't be much income to further support any contributions in this corpus after that point. So, we will invest this money for another 15 years, and without adding further contributions, this amount will grow organically and create a sizable corpus.

Like the first corpus, this one too has two constituents – one is Employee Provident Fund (EPF) and the other is the National Pension Scheme (NPS). The employee Provident Fund is meant to ensure capital protection along with a decent rate of return. While NPS is intended to bring a better return. Cost-effectiveness and tight control around NPS investments will ensure the return is decent with reduced exposure to risk. Again, it is not expected to add further contributions beyond early retirement but one can always add any extra money to the NPS pot.

Assumptions

There are a few assumptions in the calculation of the 25x rule. For example, inflation has been considered at 4%. Inflation is often higher in a developing country like India, but it is expected that as the economy matures, the general rate of inflation over one's lifetime will decrease. One can also argue this based on the current inflation rate, which is on the higher side at the time of writing this book. Though the current inflation is currently high, it won't remain high; it rises and falls over time. We based our 4% inflation rate on the average of upper and lower tolerance limits as specified by the Reserve Bank of India's target rate of inflation.

The expected rate of return is assumed as 12%. Though, in the last few decades, several equity mutual funds have consistently given a return of more than 15%. We are using 12% to be on the safer side, considering potential market conditions during accumulation or at the time of early retirement.

The current expenses are the baseline for calculating future expenses based on the general rise in the price of goods and services. Though the actual situation could vary, having this defined approach will help you avoid surprises at the onset of early retirement. At that point, there may be further reduction in some of the expenses but there could be additions as well. So, the expenses have been assumed to be the same. The key here is that one will maintain one's old lifestyle. There will not be any major changes in that.

Constituents of Retirement Kitty

The portfolio should be structured around various types of asset classes. The core of the portfolio should be around EPF (Employee Provident Fund) & PPF (Public Provident Fund). These two instruments are debt/bond, based on the characteristics of the safety of capital along with a predictable rate of return. The EPF and the PPF will ensure the core is always sturdy and not prone to capital loss at any time. This can always form 30 to 40% of the overall retirement corpus.

The EPF and the PPF are products backed by the Government of India and are assured in terms of capital protection and interest offered. Though the interest rate could fluctuate over time, the current offered rate, as well as the historically offered rate, are excellent. They can't be matched with any other products given their safety.

One should utilize the full limit (tax-free) offered by EPF which is currently 2.5 lacs per annum. If the actual EPF contribution is less than this limit, the additional sum can be contributed through VPF (Voluntary Provident Fund). The maturity of EPF could be event-based, and you can take it based on events like medical emergencies or job changes. Essentially, the corpus of EPF could be accessed early and should form the core building block of your retirement corpus, though not necessarily of early retirement.

Public Provident Fund is the second block of the core building block of retirement corpus. One should utilize the absolute limit of investing 1.5 Lacs per year. As the maturity of this product is 15 years, putting 1.5 lacs per year for 15 years will create a sturdy amount that is not prone to any market fluctuations.

If one utilizes the full limit of 1.5 lacs per annum for 15 years, one can accumulate around 40 lacs in PPF based on the current rate of interest of 7.1%. The predictability of return along with capital safety is a key characteristic of this product. Therefore, this is another important product for early retirement.

The next layer should come from the National Pension System (NPS). Though NPS may not be beneficial for early retirement, it can create a good corpus once one has attained the retirement age defined by the NPS system. Though the returns offered by NPS may not match some of the leading mutual funds, the real beauty of NPS lies in its cost-effectiveness, additional tax benefits offered during accumulation, and partially available tax-free amount at the onset of retirement.

Contribution to NPS is included in Tier 1 accounts, and the maturity amount is available at age 60 and cannot be accessed prior. This is beneficial as you will have money specifically intended as a retirement corpus at the age of 60. This will ensure that your money is well-invested, keeping a long-term view of the investment horizon, and allowing your money time to compound. Remember, compounding is the only magic in the investment world; the rest are simply tricks.

The framework and design of NPS ensure that the cost of investing in NPS is highly cost-effective in comparison to mutual funds. NPS cost structure is the least, not only in India but throughout the world. In other words, NPS is one of the cheapest products in the pension world. Whereas in actively managed mutual funds, the expense ratio could be more than 1-2%, NPS has costs attached far below this 1%. On average the cost of 1 to 1.5% is saved in NPS compared to actively managed mutual funds. This cost-saving may look insignificant in the short term but after a decade, it will make a huge difference for the corpus.

NPS is tightly regulated with very little chance of irregularity in fund management. There are several rules and guidelines set by PFRDA (The Pension Fund Regulatory & Development Authority) for fund managers, ensuring that pensioners' rights are protected. The simplicity of NPS also lies in its asset classes. These include Equity, Corporate debt, Government Bonds, and Alternative Investment Funds. These are basic asset classes and do not include any derivative-based products, ensuring the basic safety net is applied to the investments by avoiding reckless and risky bets.

At the onset of retirement at the age of 60 (as per the current rules), the availability of funds is cost-effective. 60% of the corpus could be accessed in a lump sum and it is tax-free, while the remaining 40% could be used to buy an annuity from an insurance company. If we compare this tax-free 60% with withdrawal from similar mutual funds, tax savings are high as you will have to pay 10% long-term capital gain tax on any capital appreciation above 1 lac on your mutual funds' profit.

Next are a couple of mutual fund schemes that offer far superior returns than other investment layers previously discussed. The focus should be to identify and keep invested in equity-based mutual funds. These should be a combination of consistently performing diversified equity mutual funds, balance advantage funds, and Equity based hybrid funds in the early accumulation phase. At later stages, such as a few years before the onset of early retirement, begin putting money in hybrid debt funds.

Let's understand the benefit of such funds concerning retirement. A good set of diversified equity funds in the initial stages of accumulation should be utilized as there are still 10-15 years until early retirement. It has been observed that equity mutual funds perform well over the long term. Generally, over this period, there could be 2 to 3 market cycles that could be easily utilized by the fund in its favor. The mode of investments should be systematic, such as investing a fixed sum over a defined frequency. There could also be opportunities when the stock market is not performing well. One could then consider adding lumpsum to the same fund.

Balance advantage funds are funds where fund managers choose the allocation of equity, bond, etc., based on market conditions. For example, when the market is at its peak, the fund manager of a balanced advantage fund could sell some of the equity shares and move the money into debt or money market instruments. This is an active way of managing allocations across various asset classes to prevent or reduce losses when the stock market is at its peak. When the equity market is in the bear phase and many quality stocks are available cheaply or at a reasonable price, the fund manager can move investments from debt to Equity. Essentially, fund managers decide where to allocate the money based on prevailing market conditions. These types of funds are also called Dynamic Asset Allocation mutual funds.

Equity-based hybrid funds are funds where the majority of the money is put into Equity. Let's say 70% of the fund is in Equity while the remaining is in debt, including money market instruments. These have good exposure to Equities but also have 20-30% in debt, which is a cushion in a falling market. The exposure to such funds in the early and middle part of the accumulation phase gives good returns along with some cushioning against any fall in the market.

The last category is Debt Hybrid Funds. These are the funds that primarily invest in debt or bonds with some exposure in equity. Let's say debt hybrid funds invest 75-80% in debt funds and the remaining, around 20%, are in Equity. Such funds are good in the late accumulation phase where one can start adding fresh money into this while systematically transferring funds out of diversified equity and equity-based hybrid funds.

The beauty of these funds lies in their capital protection characteristics along with lifting the overall return due to exposure to Equity. These funds will generate stable income via investments in debts or bonds while benefitting from any positive movement in the price of equities. Even if the equity market is not doing well, the overall exposure of such debt-based hybrid funds is around 20% so, the loss is minimized. Let's take a bear market scenario where the market index is down by 30% and these funds perform exactly like the market index. The losses of the fund will be 20% to 30% of the overall fund. This would be 6% of the overall fund and the positive performance of debt funds would cover some or all of such losses.

Another category of funds where you can put in some of your money is Index Funds. Index funds are well known and invested in by many investors in developed countries, especially the USA. It is often said that the majority of actively managed funds are not able to beat the returns given by the Index. This is due to the size and maturity of markets in those countries. There are costs associated with the frequent buying and selling of stocks in actively managed funds. With Index funds, they are bought and sold only when a change in Index composition occurs, which is not often.

In India, Index funds are not popular since many actively managed funds beat the return offered by Index funds. However, in the last few years, various asset management companies have launched several Index funds, and demand for such funds has increased. These funds are low in cost and are expected to be at par in the future in terms of returns.

Consider looking at a couple of Index based funds for retirement purposes. You can choose a good fund based on the Nifty 100 Index and Nifty Midcap 150 index. The criteria should be how the fund is performing in comparison to the Index it is tracking. Along with performance, you should also look at the cost of investing in an Index fund. For cost comparison purposes, one can look at the Expense Ratio of the funds being compared. The lower the expense ratio, the better the cost-effectiveness of the fund.

Let's summarise the key structure of the portfolio, including the core portfolio and the ones in the periphery.

> ### Employee Provident Fund / Voluntary Provident Fund (EPF/VPF):

> The contribution in EPF will be before in-hand salary and includes employer contribution. It is assumed for the given example that one can contribute 10-15 thousand per month. As part of

building a retirement corpus, we will be investing in this for another 15 years until the usual retirement date. This corpus is not intended for early retirement. If 12000 Rs per month is considered as EPF contribution, this will reach approximately 40 lacs at the assumed rate of 7.5% per annum after 15 years, which is our intended early retirement. However, we will not use this money for early retirement and will keep it for another 15 years. As the period is now 30 years, the interest rate will decrease with an assumed average rate of return of 6%. After 30 years, this will total 1 Cr.

➢ **Public Provident Fund (PPF):**

Though the limit of investing PPF is 1.5 lacs per annum, in this example, we are assuming that 1.2 lacs per annum will be contributed. At the current rate of interest of 7.1%, one will accumulate a few lacs above 30 lacs. As the maturity of PPF is around 15 years, we could take out this money and use it as part of the early retirement corpus.

➢ **National Pension Scheme (NPS):**

We intend to contribute 5000 Rs per month and the corpus will be around 25 lacs. As there is a limit of withdrawal on the tier 1 account of NPS, we will be invested in NPS with no further contributions. Even if we don't contribute anything after early retirement, these 25 lacs will become 1.35 Cr, as the assumed rate of return is 12%. Availability of NPS funds is in a tax-effective way and can be utilized at the start of the usual retirement age of 60.

➢ **Mutual Funds:**

This is one of the instruments where we are trying to beat inflation by a good margin to ensure that the future value of money is in our favor. One is suggested to invest around 10,000 Rs per month for the next 15 years. As we discussed earlier, the type of mutual funds should be one of the following – Diversified Equity Fund, Balance Advantage Fund, Hybrid Equity Fund, or Hybrid Debt Funds. Again the utilization of the above should depend on whether you are in the early, middle, or late accumulation phase or the distribution phase. The first three funds are advised to start in the accumulation phase. The last one is intended for the distribution phase. Any additional contributions in the late accumulation phase should still go into the Hybrid Equity Fund. Short to medium-term investments, at least for retirement purposes, should not go to primarily equity funds.

If the issue is with discipline in terms of investing money into SIPs for retirement purposes, a specific set of retirement-based solution funds could be chosen. Several Retirement based solutions are simply diversified equity or hybrid funds. Generally, these funds have a lock-in period before you can redeem them. Alternatively, redemption is discouraged before retirement with added exit loads. Though it is not necessary to use these funds, they could be considered since they are labeled Retirement Fund. This can help you not be influenced to redeem them before your intended retirement.

While these funds may not give you the best returns in their category, their risk-reward is balanced. These funds invest with the objective of long-term return and are best for value investing. Also, due to the retirement objective, unnecessary and risky bets are avoided.

Index funds and retirement-based solution funds are meant to be part of equity diversified funds in our recommended types of mutual funds and should not be confused with a new category of recommended funds.

Identifying a good mutual fund

There are many criteria to consider when identifying a good fund. We will discuss some of the prominent ones. It is assumed that we have already identified the category of mutual funds based on the suggestions in this book. For example, we need to identify a good Equity based Hybrid fund. Before we look at the fund selection criteria, let's look at some of the important things to consider.

➢ Avoid any funds offered during New Fund Offer (NFO) as these funds do not have any historical performance. Though historical performance may not be replicated in the future, the record of the fund, its style, and returns provide some historical reference. As a thumb rule, don't look at funds less than 3 years old.

➢ Always invest directly via AMCs and especially via a direct plan. There are always differences in return offered by regular plans vs direct plans. Direct plans always offer a better return. There is an additional return of around 0.50% to 1% while investing direct plan. Regular plans are chosen when the investment decision or execution is helped by an intermediary, like a broker or distributor.

Now let's discuss how to identify a good mutual fund and what criteria are worth looking at.

Fund Portfolio and Diversification:
Though the broader contours of fund objectives are already defined, one needs to look at the diversification of securities of the fund. There

should not be concentrated allocation of funds into a few securities. The diversification across sectors also matters a lot as a particular theme may not perform over the long term so diversification across various sectors becomes necessary. One should be aware of over-diversification which can become a drag on the fund.

Fund performance:
This is the most important criterion evaluated. However, these criteria should be looked at along with the other criteria. One should look at the return offered by a fund from 3 months, 6 months, 1 year, 3 years, 5 years, 7 years, and the inception perspective. Instead of absolute return, one should look at annualized return for the period given above. Also, the performance should be judged against the benchmark index along with peer funds in the same category. The comparison could be done to see how this fund has performed concerning category average.

Fund Manager and its style:
The record of the fund managers must be thoroughly checked and their past and currently managed funds should be looked at. One should be aware at least from a historical perspective how various funds of the fund manager have performed. Also, it is good to know their style of investment. For example, active or passive.

A fund manager could be a frequent buyer and seller of securities which could add further cost and drain the fund. Also, it may mean a lack of conviction. A fund manager may be known to be biased towards a particular sector, so it's important to take a cautious look at the funds managed by a fund manager.

Fund Size:
Several funds have a very low fund size and offer attractive returns. However, these may be risky as such funds generate an extra return by taking extra risks which may not be needed. Also, the very large size of a fund may become a drag on the fund due to its sheer size. Such bulky funds are overcrowded with investments and they lose agility so slow down in performance. There are limited securities in the Indian stock market especially the ones with good liquidity so a fund is forced to buy the same securities or buy a larger number of securities causing over-diversification. There are exceptions to such scenarios but one has to look at these criteria while evaluating a fund. A good fund and fund manager limits the investment when it becomes big to protect the interest of the existing investor and keep the high performance of the fund.

Expense ratio:
This is one of the important factors when choosing a factor. One should always compare the expense ratio as the expense ratio of actively managed funds varies a lot. For example, a fund with a 0.50% lower expense ratio than another fund with similar returns creates a significant difference over a long period.

Asset Management Company's (AMC) Track record:
There are various investment models and processes adopted by AMCs when deciding on investments. Certain AMCs have a superior model for such decision-making. We as an investor may not have the details of those models but high-level principles are available to look at and are evident from the performance of the funds. The majority of the funds of an AMC in a particular category perform well above the category average. This is

due to their methodology and models, which they have developed within their investment decisions.

Identifying a good health insurance policy

There are many factors one should look for before buying a health insurance policy. Here are a few prominent factors one should consider before buying a health insurance policy.

Buying early:
There are many benefits of buying health insurance early namely low premiums and serving the waiting periods during your young age when you may not have a claim, Better and wider coverage, discount in premium when no claim are a few benefits when you buy a health insurance policy in your early age.

Buy what you need:
Look at what could be your medical requirements and chose the plan which matches to your need and covers wider issues and has many benefits. Some of the benefits you could look for are inpatient hospitalization including pre and post-hospitalization, daycare coverage, ambulance, etc.

You should always prioritize plan benefits over the price of the plan. Disclose all your medical history to avoid any claim rejection at later date.

Choose the right policy type:
If you are an individual with no family responsibility, go for an individual health insurance plan. If you have a family with kids, choose a family floater policy with maximum benefits. The policy should come with lifelong renewability as you would not want any rejection during your old age when buying an afresh policy.

Network hospital coverage:
Always check network hospital coverage for a given health insurance provider. A health insurer with wider coverage of network hospitals is always good to go for. Also, ensure that the cashless option is available as arranging cash at the time of emergencies is not easy and full of inconvenience.

Restrictions:
This is one of the important factors one should look at it. Look at the waiting period for Pre-existing disease existing to know your exact eligibility for coverage. A lower waiting period is better always. There are limits for room rent, ambulance, surgical procedure, etc. So, look for higher limits to avoid any hidden expenses. A careful comparison of these limits at the time of buying health insurance is essential to avoid any surprises during claims.

Also, look for a co-payment feature under which the policyholder has to pay a fixed amount if there is a claim, this amount should be comparatively lower. These are also called excess as this excess amount has to be borne by the policyholder during a claim. Any amount above this excess will be paid by the health insurance provider.

There are also exclusions for each health insurance plan which specify which illnesses or diseases are not covered. One has to be mindful of such exclusions and choose a plan with fewer exclusions.

Comparing quotes online and buying online:
Request quotes from a couple of online portals and compare them and choose the one which suits you in terms of features. Buying online is always cheaper. The same health insurance features are sold at different premiums by different online portals. Don't compromise on your plan

features but choose the policy with a lower premium.

Claim settlement ratio:
Always look for a health insurance company with a higher Claim Settlement Ratio as this means that your chances of getting a claim are better. This is one of the important factors when buying a health insurance policy and should never be ignored.

Summary of Contributions and expected corpus

Let's summarise the contributions made to various buckets and the corpus at early retirement and usual retirement age –

Early retirement:

PPF: Per month Contribution – 10,000 Rs, Assumed Rate of Return 7%, Timeframe – 15 years, Corpus – 30 Lacs.

Mutual Fund SIP: Per month Contribution – 10,000 Rs, Assumed Rate of Return 12%, Timeframe – 15 years, Corpus – 50 Lacs.

Mutual fund Lumpsum: Lumpsum Contribution – Rs 5 lacs, Assumed Rate of Return 15%, Timeframe – 15 years, Corpus – 40 Lacs.

Total Contribution per month (excluding Lumpsum) – 20,000 Rs, **Total Corpus** – Rs 1.2 Cr.

Retirement at Usual Age:

EPF: Per month Contribution – 12,000 Rs, Assumed Rate of Return 7.50%, Contribution

Timeframe – 15 years, Corpus after 30 years – Rs 1.20 Cr.

NPS SIP: Per month Contribution – 5,000 Rs, Assumed Rate of Return 12%, Contribution Timeframe – 15 years, Corpus after 30 years – Rs 1.35 Cr.

Total Contribution per month (excluding Lumpsum) – 17,000 Rs, **Total Corpus** – Rs 2.55 Cr.

Questions?

One can ask several questions about the overall approach. Let's discuss some of the obvious ones. How one can contribute 25K each month for retirement purposes in the given salary of 1 lacs along with 5 lacs of lumpsum investments? One will have additional expenses like buying a house, owning a car, children's education, etc.

Yes, 25K per month may sound too much initially unless you have made up your mind that you want to go for early retirement. The reason for high contributions is that we are trying to make the most of the time before retirement. One has to be ready for some of the inconveniences for a great deal of financial freedom. There is a simple way of saving more – reduce expenses. We tend to ignore the basic fact that reducing expenses is the only way for creating wealth and getting on early retirement. This is the first part of guaranteeing wealth. The other is saving and putting your savings to bring and create more money.

Often, people think that wealth is about being rich and that a wealthy person is synonymous with a rich person. But that's not always true. Richness is more materialistic and often associated with flashiness while wealth is spiritual and it's hidden many a time. But the real peace of financial freedom lies with the wealthy not necessarily with the rich.

As we said earlier, we need to reduce our expenses, save money, and put it to work. Budgeting could be an effective way of saving more, keeping track of all expenses, and getting rid of unnecessary ones is the key here. You could put aside 25K per month on the very first few days of the month after you receive your month-end salary of Rs 1 Lac. Then you could plan how to could live on the remaining 75K. Go through your expense list for a few months and see what is draining your savings and plug those gaps. Remember, you can always look for alternative cheaper options. There are several systematic ways of reducing expenses – look for renting a cheaper house. You just need to go away a bit from the City center. Drive less and use more public transportation, reduce eating outside, etc. Your ways of reducing expenses could vary significantly from the ones suggested here.

Coming back to collecting 5 lacs for lumpsum investments is easier. Go back to section – 'Saving mindset for early retirement' and any savings suggested there put it in one place, one can save this amount in the next 2-3 years. But this needs financial discipline and eagerness to save.

Though we assumed that the current salary is 1 lac per month, this does not mean it won't increase further. So, it's not only expenses that are going to increase but your salary will too. You can always work on your skill set and look for better-paying opportunities. Regular Salary increments along with an increase in pay due to Job hopping will create an additional pool of money that could be used for other purposes. We are not accommodating such increments for the contribution of our early retirement. So, a 25K contribution may look like 25% of your post-tax salary in the first year but due to salary increment, this percentage will go down as your salary increases every year. Who knows if you focus on this part, 5-7 years down the line, your 25K contribution could be 15% or less of the overall salary.

Does the rate of return look too optimistic?

Yes, they do look optimistic, but the future could be better or worse. It's just we have to be ready for all possibilities. The rate of return taken for all the instruments meant for retirement are the average historical rate of return. If you look at the mutual funds' history. Several funds have given consistently a 17 to 18% rate of return over 10 and 20 years. Our model takes 12% which is a bit conservative.

Onset of Retirement

At Early Retirement

This is the time when we want to enjoy the fruits of our investments and look forward to a new life and routine. From a financial perspective, there are two phases of early retirement – one is the transition phase and the second is actual early retirement. Let's first discuss a few things. As mentioned, early retirement does not mean halting income-generating activities. You will be able to leave your regular job that funded your lifestyle and try something new.

Now you can pick up something you like to do. It does not have to be regular; it may be one's hobby that one can pursue and generate some income. You can go for charity or volunteer work, or you can start a small business that does not require much capital. Essentially, one can do anything without bothering much about the income generated by it. The purpose of doing something should be known, and there should be engagement with the community and people around.

In terms of the financial aspect, during the transition phase, one can transfer Equity based mutual funds corpus into debt-based hybrid funds systematically. So, over three to five years, all the money invested in equity-based mutual funds should be transferred to Hybrid Debt Fund. This can be done via a Systematic Transfer Plan (STP) from Equity to Debt Hybrid. This STP can start a couple of years before early retirement and should continue a few years post early retirement.

For early retirement, one can withdraw a sum equivalent to one's expenses every month from the Hybrid Debt fund. This can be set up on monthly basis as a Systematic Withdrawal Plan. So, on a fixed date, a fixed sum of money will be transferred from the Hybrid Debt fund to one's savings account.

We calculated the corpus from Mutual funds both SIP and Lumpsum will be around 90 lacs and the corpus from PPF is 30 lacs. This makes total availability of 1.20 Cr at the start of early retirement. The first year's expenses are 8.65 lacs, which means monthly expenses of Rs 72,000. Assuming that one is earning a return of 9% per annum in a Hybrid Debt Fund, and his expenses are increasing 4% rate, which is the same as the inflation rate.

With early retirement, one can start withdrawing Rs 72000 per month in the first month and increase the withdrawal amount by 4% per year accounting for the increase in the cost of living. There are two ways to set your withdrawal.

With the first method, one can spread this increase of 4% per year on monthly basis. If the first month's withdrawal is Rs 72000 then 2nd month's withdrawal would be Rs72240 (72000+ (72000*4%)/12). This is nothing but last month's withdrawal + an Increase of 4% per annum/12.

The second method is to increase the withdrawal amount by 4% per year on annual basis. For example, the first year's withdrawal will be Rs 72000 per month for the year and it will be the same for all 12 months of the first year. The second year's withdrawal will be Rs 74880 per month for the whole year. This calculation is – Rs 72000 + (72000 * 4%).

Again, one can always set up this as a Systematic Withdrawal Plan (SWP) with a step amount of 4% every year. The withdrawal amount based on this 4% increase will be around Rs 131000 per month in the 15th year. Even if you have taken the withdrawal from this corpus of Rs 1.2 Cr for 15 years, you will be surprised to know that you still have around Rs 1.1 Cr left in your Hybrid Debt Fund. This is possible due to the rate of return earned on corpus being 9%. Even though one took out 8.65 Lacs per month in the first year but earning based on 9% was 10.8 lacs. So, the withdrawal amount was less than the earned amount.

The rate of return of 9% was taken based on the historical performance of some of the good funds over more than 10 years. And 4% was our usual inflation rate. If you want a further pessimistic scenario, then you can further decrease the rate of return to 8% and increase the inflation rate to 6%. Even with these two numbers, which are not more favorable to your corpus than the earlier numbers, you will still be left with 25 Lacs in your corpus. The idea was to survive for 15 years with the saved money meant for early retirement and we can see from the above illustrations that there is still money left in the corpus. In an optimistic and practical sense, one still has got Rs 1.1 Cr corpus left meant for early retirement. And in a bit pessimistic scenario, we still have Rs 25 Lacs unspent.

There are several websites you can use for SWP calculation. Look for the calculator which includes the inflation rate to accommodate the increase in the cost of living.

At Usual Retirement

For the usual retirement at the age of 60 years i.e. after 15 years of onset of early retirement, one has the corpus of Rs 1.20 Cr from EPF and around 80 lacs (60% of NPS corpus as Lumsum) from NPS. So, in total, we have Rs 2 Cr for the rest of life. Additionally, we have some left over from the early retirement along with 40% of NPS corpus in form of Annuity. Let's see first how much income the NPS annuity part of the corpus could generate. You could go to LIC's website and use the calculator to calculate the pension. Here we are taking the example of 60 years of age and Jeevan Akshay Pension plan with immediate annuity for life. This turns out to be Rs 35000 per month.

Based on the same data we used for the calculation of expenses at the time of early retirement, we will calculate the expenses at the age of 60 years i.e. 15 years after early retirement. We will baseline our earlier calculation of 8.65 Lacs per annum as the expense at the onset of early retirement.

At the age of 60 years, the expenses will be 15.60 Lacs per annum i.e. Rs 1.3 Lacs per month for the first year and we are assuming that this will increase by 4%. Again, we will transfer a part of the money from EPF and the lumpsum part of NPS into a Hybrid Debt fund and start an SWP of Rs. 1.3 Lacs with a step-up amount of 4% per annum basis. One could use either model of spreading the increase of yearly expenses same as we used at the time of early retirement systematic withdrawal.

In the total corpus, we have 1.2 Cr from EPF plus 80 lacs from NPS lumpsum plus 1 Cr from leftover from early retirement. So, we have a total of Rs 3 Cr as retirement corpus along with a monthly pension of Rs 35000 from the NPS annuity option.

To eliminate systematic or market risk, we will invest 2 Cr into Government securities which are available for retail investors now. These are risk-free securities where the government pays a fixed amount of interest rate on quarterly/half yearly/yearly basis. If we assume the current and past rates as an indication, one can expect a coupon of 7.5% per annum on a 20-year long-term bond. We are assuming that one will be invested until maturity. So, on maturity, one will get the total invested money back. The coupons or interest rate on Rs 2 Cr will turn out to be 15 Lacs per annum which is almost the same as the expense at the age of 60 years. So, monthly income from Govt securities' interest will be around Rs 1.25 Lacs.

So, income at the start of 60 years is now 1.25 Lacs + 35K. I.e. Rs 1.60 Lacs while the expenses are Rs. 1.3 Lacs, So, the saving for Rs 30k should go into a good hybrid fund. This saving of Rs 30K will go down every year due to the increase. So, the income from NPS annuity and interest from long-term Govt Bonds will suffice for 5 to 6 years and in these 5 years, there will be additions of Rs. 3.6 Lacs in a hybrid fund, Rs 3 lacs second year, 2.4 Lacs third year, and so on... This sum invested in a good hybrid fund will be around 10 to 12 lacs.

Remember, we have not used our corpus of Rs 1 Cr from the hybrid debt fund which we invested at the age of 60 years age. If we add savings of above 10 lacs, we have a corpus of 1.1 Cr. But hold on, we need to also add any interest earned on 1 Cr in the last 5-6 years after the age of 60 years. So, we assume a rate of return of 9%, this will turn to Rs 1.5 Cr. The total in the hybrid fund will be Rs 1.6 Cr after adding 10 lacs. Essentially at the age of 65 years, one has an income of Rs 1.6 Lacs from NPS annuity and Long term Govt bonds. Any shortfall in income could be withdrawn from Rs 1.6 Cr. This will ensure that one has sufficient money for one's expenses. At the age of 80, there will be a return of Rs 2 Cr from maturity of Govt bonds, and Rs 35000 per month is for a lifetime. The value in the hybrid debt fund will be well over 1 Cr.

In a nutshell, one will be able to live life comfortably from a financial perspective and will leave an inheritance for the next generation.

There are a couple of things to be mindful of. For example, one should spread the money meant for a hybrid debt fund into multiple hybrid debt funds to spread the risks. One should always review the performance of funds every couple of years. If a particular fund is lagging and is not able to generate the above category return for 2 to 3 years, one should move to a better-performing fund. Moving to a better-performing fund is always a better deal than sticking to a non-performing fund. One can always use the help of a Certified Financial Planner to select funds based on their needs.

If the interest rate offered by Long term Govt bonds is not attractive enough at one's age of 60 years as these returns are today. One can always look for safer options like annuities offered by insurance companies or any other pension options offered by the government. The key here is that one's priority should be capital protection.

Finally

The key to early retirement is early savings, being thrifty, considerate in expenses, alternative thinking, capital protection approach, patience, and most importantly flexibility in approach. These values will help you to achieve your early retirement and to be financially free. Remember, every person is unique and so the approach to early retirement will be unique to everybody though one can use the same framework and modify it to suit its situation.

Remember the key to early retirement lies in 3Ms – Maximum Savings, Managing Risks, and Magic of Compounding. One has to inculcate the value of being thrifty, this is something that will always be on your side be it a good time or a bad time. Being thrifty does not mean being stingy but being considerate in one's spending. The spending should be driven by the simple idea of whether this is going to create value or not. Being thrifty is a core Indian middle-class value and we have possessed this quality for generations but have been succumbing to consumerism these days. The access to social media and the globalized world has instigated us to shun our value of being thrifty.

Consumerism is good for the economy but not at the cost of future generations. One has to be always mindful of one's lifestyle. Instead one should focus on sustainability at the individual level. Remember, you always have a choice, always explore that when it comes to consumption of the modern world's goods and services.

Taking too many risks is not good for your financial health, there should be a disciplined approach to define how much risk one can take at a given time. Remember, take only those risks which you can bear in the worst-case scenario. Don't explore the risk at a superficial level but go deeper to figure out the damage it can cause and the rewards it brings up for you.

I hope this book has given you enough thought to begin exploring various possibilities for a life free of financial independence.

About Author

Abhishek has been an Investment professional throughout and comes from a family engaged in the financial advisory profession. He has worked for many Investment Managers across India and the UK. He holds a post-graduate diploma in Finance and Insurance from National Insurance Academy, Pune, and could be reached at abhimis14@gmail.com.

www.ingramcontent.com/pod-product-compliance
Lightning Source LLC
Chambersburg PA
CBHW071123240526
45465CB00023B/788